RAILWAY HERITAGE
DAWN OF THE DIESELS
1956-66
Part 2

RAILWAY HERITAGE

DAWN OF THE DIESELS
1956-66
Part 2

First-generation diesel locomotives and units captured by the camera of

John Spencer Gilks

Edited by Mike Esau

SLP

Silver Link Publishing Ltd

First published in October 1998

British Library Cataloguing in Publication Data

A catalogue record for this book is available from the British Library.

ISBN 1 85794 110 1

Silver Link Publishing Ltd
The Trundle
Ringstead Road
Great Addington
Kettering
Northants NN14 4BW

The number appended to each caption is the negative number. Requests for prints may be made via the Publishers.

Printed and bound in Great Britain

Half title **Leaderfoot Viaduct, Borders; Class 08, St Boswells-Greenlaw freight, 18 July 1963.**
Much controversy surrounded the possibility of demolition of this elegant structure, which was of no use to BR following withdrawal of this goods service to Greenlaw in 1965. Eventually it was to set a precedent for the retention of disused viaducts by being put under the wing of Historic Scotland. *2917*

Page 2 **Quy, Cambridgeshire; German railbus, 4.21 pm Cambridge-Mildenhall, 21 March 1962.**
The village is Stow-cum-Quy, but presumably the railway authorities thought this too complex. I'm in the car and have visited Ridgmont station and looked at the line in Bedford, Sandy and Cambridge before arriving here. Obviously the train had to return from Mildenhall and I also saw it at Isleham passing a tall Great Eastern lower-quadrant signal. In recent times I have used a coach company here for field visits with weekend courses at Madingley Hall.

The Mildenhall branch had been allowed to deteriorate by the time of my picture at Quy, to such an extent that all the hinges had worn away on the adjacent level crossing gates (over a farm track). The gates were held to the posts by string, and the porter lifted them off and pulled them across the lane when the train was signalled. Thus was the condition of some branch lines by the time railbuses sought to rescue them from possible closure. Quy closed in 1962 (two years later for goods). *2591*

Below **Polquhap, Strathclyde; Class 45 and LMS Class '5' 4-6-0, 4.10 pm Glasgow (St Enoch)-Leeds, 15 April 1965.**
This picture is taken between Cumnock and New Cumnock on the Glasgow & South Western main line and shows the afternoon train from Glasgow to Leeds at a time of transition. The service continued from Carlisle over the Settle route. It used to make one round trip each weekday, leaving Leeds at 10.25 am. Today most trains, 'Sprinter' units, are limited to Glasgow/Carlisle, with the addition of the Stranraer/Newcastle through trains. *AL*

Opposite **Allington Junction, Lincolnshire; Class 25, Nottingham (Victoria)-Skegness, 10 July 1965.**
Allington Junction is the gateway to the Lincolnshire coast, notably Skegness. Here trains from Nottingham and the East Midlands turn left to avoid Grantham and reversal there. It has assumed a new importance in recent years with electrification of the East Coast Main Line (ECML) and the break-up of the network into separate companies under privatisation. The signal box is of Great Northern design. *3474*

CONTENTS

INTRODUCTION

Lineside features fascinate me. There are mileposts, for instance, that owe the distance they record to the company that built the railway rather than the current point of departure and destination. Just a few in the West Country and on the Settle & Carlisle line top the 300 mark. Some are very distinctive, such as those in the North East, where the quarter-miles are marked by one, two or three additional cast iron pointers.

On one of my many journeys from King's Cross to York an old lady sitting opposite commented on the speed we were travelling. We were able to look at the time, see that we were just an hour from London, and spot the 99 milepost near Stoke Summit. She was amazed and favourably impressed. I'm sure that few rail passengers realise that at times they are moving at more than two miles a minute.

Other lineside features seen through the carriage window are gradient posts, speed restriction signs, level crossings and a whole variety of railway buildings from the most handsome station to the humblest cottage. Semaphore signals and signal boxes are now more hard to come by, though they sometimes surprise when they appear betwixt modernisation schemes. At one time you would see loading gauges, cattle docks and marshalling yards, large and small. Bridges, viaducts and tunnels (which give welcome respite from those addicted to mobile phones) are better seen from the car.

It is this myriad of features that I hope to portray in my photography, sometimes focused in on the milepost and at other times opened up on the landscape. And because so much has disappeared from the railway scene of the 1950s and '60s there is a great deal of interest to see and discuss. Had I foreseen the future I would have picked up the

station nameboards and other paraphernalia in the debris of disused lines that I used to walk amongst with my camera, and would have made my fortune selling them today!

Such sales are frequented by the general public as much as the enthusiast. It has become fashionable to have some railwayana in the drawing room. If nothing else it is a talking point for visitors. In my view these are the people most likely now to buy railway books and videos. I notice that the fanatical enthusiast has disappeared from my weekend schools; instead there is the person seeking to revive happy nostalgic memories, and the social historian, those wanting to know more about their locality and how this was influenced by the railway. In putting together this book I have had them very much in mind, and hope that they will enjoy it as much as the erstwhile train-spotter.

Peter Handford, the distinguished sound recordist of trains, writing to me as long ago as March 1961 about letters sent to him in the light of a newspaper article, said that they proved 'what I have long suspected, that railway enthusiasts are not interested in records, and the only people that are interested in them are the much more abstract type of people who just love railways but are not necessarily informed or enthusiasts'. They marvel at the self-discipline of railwaymen in a country where individual freedom is exploited. As I understand it, Silver Link Publishing, through The Nostalgia Collection, is focusing on this market and I am grateful to them for promoting this book with those folk in mind.

It goes without saying that I am greatly indebted to Mike Esau once more for his painstaking work in producing excellent prints from my negatives and those of Alan Lillywhite (prefixed 'AL' in the captions).

The coming of the diesel and the going of the steam locomotive changed the railway scene in the UK for ever. The period in question overlapped Beeching with the Government's reshaping of the railway map, and together they provided me with a challenge: to travel

Opposite page **Yealmpton, Devon; Class 119, 11.45 am Exeter Central-Yealmpton, 11 April 1959.**
These two views show the Railway Enthusiasts Club 'Devon Rambler' tour. The station had closed to passengers as early as 1947, and was to close to goods traffic in 1960. *1570/1569*

the railway network by train and car with my camera as comprehensively and quickly as possible. My Wolseley 1500 GPJ 3C covered 36,000 miles in 18 months! The result was early diesel locomotives and multiple units illustrated on cross-country and branch lines that have long since disappeared. When others put their cameras away because the steam locomotive was their prime concern, mine remained in full use to record the changing scene. Alan went on more organised railtours than I did in latter years, and his negatives are a valuable archive of a period that has virtually finished.

As I have said before, in my experience railwaymen became markedly divided in the Beeching era between those who saw the world of politics - and a closure programme - as the route to promotion, and those who loved what they did, took pride in it for its own sake, and wanted it to continue. The national politicians had divided and ruled in the traditional manner. But I believe in a strange sort of way that democracy may have been the winner. We may have lost the trains, but the ways of

government have been scrutinised by the public - through an enhanced media - to a greater extent since Beeching, as they come to realise that they have been taken for a ride. Hindsight is a great educator, especially in an age of photography, video and tape recordings.

Privatisation is a natural development of the political railwaymen and it remains to be seen what comes next. Will it be innovative services with new types of train equivalent to the DMU on the Buckingham branch featured in the first volume? Or will it be an emphasis on the bottom line rather than the railway line?

Whatever happens, the railway with its private right of way into city centres must develop in this world of traffic congestion, and I hope that this book provides just a few illustrations of some of the steps that have been taken along the way to the present scene.

John Gilks
Nawton, 1998

Elmesthorpe, Leicestershire; Class 105, Leicester-Birmingham (New Street), 21 August 1961.
Although this station finally closed on 4 March 1968, trains still pass this way between the West Midlands and East Anglia. *2524*

1.
WAITING FOR THE TRAIN

The freight train that Alan, Harry and myself planned to wait for at Wearhead on 3 June 1960 never came. We had permits to travel by it but the driver thought otherwise and insisted that we went down the valley to St John's Chapel to join it there. May I explain?

The Wear Valley goods used to leave Darlington well before dawn, and as our journeys were for enjoyment we decided only to travel on its return. How to be at the head of Weardale at breakfast-time by public transport was left to me to work out. We were on one of our tours seeking to cover the BR network before closures took effect. In the event we came from Carlisle and took the afternoon train at Haltwhistle, which reversed there in making its run from Newcastle to Alston. From the terminus it was but a short walk to where Nenthead Motor Services parked their bus.

We were the subject of much interest from the local passengers when we entered the Bedford OB with our luggage. It took us very slowly up the very steep hill through the town and out across the fell to its depot in Nenthead. I had pre-arranged with the firm to take us by taxi across the watershed to the Cowshill Hotel from where we could walk down to Wearhead station in the morning. When the bus stopped, the driver took us through the garage and we emerged from the other end on a taxi ride that cost 7s 6d. We were the only guests at the hotel (there were not yet washbasins in the bedrooms) and the proprietor put on a superb five-course dinner for us. Afterwards we staggered down to the pub to find the Station Master, playing darts, who advised us that he had ordered a bag of potatoes in an effort to get the train to come. As an alternative he had laid on the BRS parcels van to take us, which, in the event, we had to use.

Some time later I learned why the engine driver had been so reluctant to come to Wearhead. Apparently a few weeks before our visit there had been no traffic beyond St John's Chapel, but a distinguished member of the Railway Club, who happened to be on the train, persuaded the driver to go ahead. During the journey a sheep was killed by the train and when the farmer submitted a claim to BR its justification was denied as no train had gone to Wearhead. When the truth was out the driver was in trouble. He was not going to be caught again with us!

The previous week we had waited for numerous trains, but on the Friday we left the train from Garsdale at Appleby, took the bus to Temple Sowerby and picked up a car I had arranged to hire from a local garage. It was a Ford Popular with only three forward gears. I had to learn to drive again and was not very competent! Next day we took the picture at Cotherstone before heading for the Deepdale and Belah Viaducts. The latter was easy of access, but I could see no way on the map of reaching Deepdale (page 84) without going along the track, so permits were obtained from the North Eastern Region allowing us to join the permanent way at Lartington station. Having toiled along the sleepers we reached a signal cabin shortly before the viaduct. Having explained why we were there to the kindly signalman, I noticed his car parked nearby.

'Oh yes,' he said. 'I come across the fields. Why don't you go and get your car and do the same; there's plenty of time before the train comes.'

And so we did. He was good enough to tell us that a banked freight would come east across Belah Viaduct at about 1 o'clock, which avoided a lot of hanging about. Crossing Deepdale required a good head for heights as there were numerous holes in the decking through which we could see the river far below.

We drove from Belah to Shap, saw the Keswick portion of 'The Lakes Express' – all maroon coaches behind a red 'Duchess' – and hurried to Appleby to meet Harry off the London train. We handed back the car on Monday, took the Lakeside goods on Tuesday, the Coniston goods on Wednesday (and the Ravenglass & Eskdale before it boasted covered coaches) and stayed overnight in Carlisle after travelling from Workington via Cockermouth (page 15). Then we were ready to go to Weardale!

At Withernsea (page13) the people are not waiting for the train but leaving it for the beach. We went back on the same DMU to Hull, from whence we had come. It was part of our August Bank Holiday weekend railtour in 1964. Harry and I left Euston on Saturday morning, transferred to the Midland upstairs at Tamworth and went via Burton-on-Trent and Walsall back to the West Coast Main Line at Rugeley. Here we watched a succession of expresses until our connection took us on to Crewe and Lancaster. There we had time to complete the circuit – Green Ayre-Wennington-Carnforth-Morecambe-Heysham-Lancaster – by a series of tight connections before returning to Preston for the night and meeting up with Alan.

Next day we all went to Leeds via Blackpool (tram to Fleetwood) and Preston-Southport direct, continuing via Wigan, Manchester, Huddersfield, Dewsbury and Batley. Bank Holiday Monday produced a through DMU from Leeds to Driffield via Selby. We sat at the back and watched the clouds of dust and leaves rise from the track behind us, as normally there was only one train each day via Bubwith at this time. We fitted in Hornsea before Withernsea and returned home via Selby and York. Then back to work for a rest!

The picture at West Kilbride (page 17) was taken while returning with the car from Northern Ireland through Stranraer and going on to Larbert for a week photographing trains in Strathmore and the lowlands.

I hope the people seen in my pictures waiting for trains enjoyed their journeys as much as we did.

County School, Norfolk; Class 101, 9.55 am Wells-next-the-Sea-Norwich, 8 August 1964.
Between Dereham and Fakenham, and until 1952 the junction for Aylsham and Wroxham, County School station has since been re-opened by preservationists. There seems to be plenty of accommodation here and the surroundings are typically Great Eastern. I'm based at Acle and will drive round North Norfolk's railways all day. The lady seems pleased to see me. *3287*

Woburn Sands, Buckinghamshire; Class 108, 6.55 pm Bletchley-Cambridge, 17 August 1963.
A few years ago I ran a weekend course at Maryland College, Woburn Sands, and asked who had come by train. Leighton Buzzard was regarded as the London railhead, and when I mentioned Woburn Sands station local students laughed and I understood why it is always under threat of closure. Yet the service is good and links straight into the Midland at Bedford. This view recalls the days when trains connected Oxford with Cambridge this way. I'm with the Kirklands returning from a morning riding in ironstone wagons at Scaldwell in Northamptonshire. Happy days! 2974

Rauceby, Lincolnshire; Class 25, Nottingham (Victoria)-Skegness, 10 July 1965.
Apart from modern signalling, lifting barriers and the station building, this line remains largely unchanged today. Skegness is the aim, although Sleaford and Boston have reason to expect passengers. I'm driving between hotels at Knipton and Tetford looking at summer Saturday extras throughout north-east Lincolnshire. There's plenty to see and enjoy. *3476*

Olney, Buckinghamshire; Class 114, 1.40 pm Bedford (Midland)-Northampton (Castle), 19 November 1960.

A wet and murky afternoon in the town where pancake racing on Shrove Tuesday causes a stir. Do notice the rolling-stock standing idly in the sidings waiting to be called as empty coaching stock (ECS) to the main line to provide excursions. So many wagons became surplus to requirements as road haulage ate into railway traffic in the 1950s and '60s that one line of the double-track section east of here to Turvey was home to them and the trains ran up and down the other track for years. Note also the complicated trackwork. 2304

Withernsea, Humberside; Class 105, 2.42 pm to Hull, 3 August 1964.

Those of you who like to trace my journeys through the pages of the book will know from the introduction to this chapter that the weekend I was in Withernsea my journey had begun at Euston and nights had been spent in Preston and Leeds. We had gone coast to coast, Blackpool to Withernsea. Look at all the people hoping to pass August Bank Holiday at the seaside. 3286

Left Moulton, North Yorkshire; Class 101, 11.43 am Darlington-Richmond, 12 April 1965.

Alan and I have ridden the train from Richmond to Darlington and back and have now returned in the car to picture the intermediate stations. This one is further from the village it is alleged to serve than Scorton, next to the west. It's a good walk from here to The Black Bull with its 'Brighton Belle' coach in which to dine. The Minister of Transport stipulated that tickets issued to service personnel at Catterick were not to be included in the revenue earned by the branch trains, so the line came to a close, despite crowds of regular passengers, in 1969. 3397

Below left Slaggyford, Northumberland; Class 101, Alston-Newcastle, 14 April 1965.

With the advent of DMUs platforms were sometimes cut back, as here, to reduce maintenance. Slaggyford – an awful name for such a lovely district – was closed in 1975, although the private replacement narrow-gauge line from Alston creeps gradually nearer. Do notice the pre-war Austin saloon on the left. 3405

Above right Haltwhistle, Cumbria; Class 101, 10.30 am Newcastle-Carlisle, 2 June 1960.

'Haltwhistle, change for Alston' reads the board, and the branch train waits on the left – it's nice to see destinations marked so clearly. I wonder what the man is putting in his pocket. An old van stands on

the right; how rarely do we see wagons standing about these days. Beside it a trailer is awaiting its prime mover. 2042

Below Cockermouth, Cumbria; Derby 'Lightweight', 5.26 pm Workington (Main)-Carlisle, 1 June 1960.

I'm travelling by this train from Workington to Carlisle and have jumped off while the parcels are being loaded. We have just seen a sign inviting us to take prime steaks in a Carlisle restaurant and our mouths are watering. 2038

Cotherstone, County Durham; Class 101, 10.00 am Middleton-in-Teesdale-Darlington, 28 May 1960.
There is quite a crowd, in their best clothes, waiting to join the through train to Barnard Castle and Darlington. Alan and I have come over the hills from Temple Sowerby in our hired Ford car and are going on to Deepdale and Belah Viaducts before picking up Harry at Appleby off 'The Waverley' express mid-afternoon. AL 1256

Kilmaurs, Strathclyde; Class 107, 3.5 pm Kilmarnock-Glasgow (St Enoch), 23 May 1964.

It's nice to see station staff, a feeling of protection and assistance sadly missed at the country station today. I have never understood why the service between Kilmarnock and Glasgow is infrequent; this was so even when the line was double-track. Now it's single between Barrhead and Kilmarnock, with just one loop at Lugton. Due to crew shortage one of our Inspection Saloon trips (see Volume 1) ran very late between Ayr and Kilmarnock, where most participants were to take the sleeper south. This was approaching Barrhead when we arrived, but the restaurant car crew were able to persuade the signalman to hold it there to give priority to the Saloons returning to Glasgow with a small contingent on board. 3185

West Kilbride, Strathclyde; Class 107, 12.45 pm Glasgow (St Enoch)-Largs, 27 August 1965.

This station is now on an electrified route from Glasgow, but only the down side has been so treated; any freight uses the more conventional arrangement. A lot of people seem to have alighted with suitcases. 3506

2.
MAIN LINE DIESELS

The media have a role in my first two pictures. I visited Doublebois during a tour of the West Country for the BBC, and carried one of their tape recorders with me. The aim was to feature the change-over from steam to diesel operation, and probably the most significant recording was made on Hemerdon bank with a diesel coupled to 'Castle' Class *Earl of Eldon* heading for Paddington. Another was made near Liskeard with a steam train climbing from Combe Junction while a diesel-hauled express passed above on the main line, one sound inserted within the other. Owing to administrative misunderstandings, both Peter Semmens and myself had been sent independently to record the Wenford Bridge goods. I finished up on Weymouth Quay with the boat train hauled by a pannier-tank complete with warning bell to clear the street ahead.

The second media connection is with the picture at Bishops Nympton & Molland. The special train 1Z48 was chartered by a company making a film with The Beatles, who are on board. This has an interesting sequel. We left immediately the train had passed and headed for our next photographic stop at South Molton station. Although this was more than a mile from the town, dozens of people were returning along the road. Thus if a remote station has something worthwhile to offer, its distance from town is not important.

Diesel-hauled trains were rare on the Minehead and Ilfracombe branches towards the end of their BR era, so holiday trains between London and the coast were important photographic opportunities. In 1970 there was one on each line – but how to see them both on the same day? It is about 45 miles from Williton station to Mortehoe station via Simonsbath. Sadly, I could not trace the precise station times of the trains, the first from Minehead, the second to Ilfracombe, but we made it with only 2 minutes to spare – and then to a point east of Mortehoe station rather than the station itself! After that we needed a rest and ambled to Umberleigh to see the return working there (page 88). What a life!

On the question of speed by road, I shall never equal the timings between Kingston-upon-Thames and Rockingham in Northamptonshire on 1 September 1962. The M1 was comparatively new, traffic congestion in North London was not yet a problem and I sailed through in a little more than 2 hours, even in my Morris Minor (although its trafficator would never fall back into place because of the slipstream). The picture at Thorpe-by-Water was one of the results.

Watton-at-Stone is a station with an interesting history. It was open for only 15 years when new with the Hertford Loop, from 2 June 1924 until 10 September 1939, a wartime casualty. Trains at this end of the line were few and far between, so when Sunday diversions from the East Coast Main Line were scheduled it was worth a visit with the camera. Then in later years electrification took place and local trains began to pass regularly through its derelict platforms en route to Stevenage New Town and Letchworth. The villagers, seeing their bus services curtailed by deregulation and yet trains going by at all hours, petitioned successfully for the trains to stop and serve them, and the station was restored. During the interim, the Railway Enthusiasts' Club had reversed a steam train there from the Hertford North direction on 15 June 1957.

By 1965 it was widely known that both the Great Central London Extension and the Somerset & Dorset were going to be closed by Beeching's masters, so I took every opportunity to visit them both by road and rail. The picture at Bruton is during one such long weekend based at Wrightlington near Radstock. The omens were not good on Saturday 27 March 1965 as we woke to find a puncture in a front tyre (and later, in Chipping Campden, had to have something else looked at) while pursuing a train to Derby hauled by *Clun Castle*, newly purchased for preservation by the late Pat Whitehouse. Our last picture that day was at Verney Junction (again!), although, had we but known, the train was to be held for some time at Ashendon Junction awaiting the passage of football specials and we might have seen it again. Instead we had dinner in Bicester and drove back to Somerset – no specific drink and drive laws in those days! – there to see on Sunday, after the call at Bruton, a special from London to Highbridge, which had come via Dorking and Bournemouth.

The picture at Ashperton was taken on the morning of the day when the last passenger trains were to serve Ross-on-Wye, and we coupled our visit with a tape recording session there in the evening, though the battery/converter did not give the Ferrograph a steady frequency.

I preceded the photo stop at Hope (page 27) with a railtour in Northern Ireland, necessitating parking

arrangements for the car in Crewe and berths on the boat from Heysham to Belfast and return.

Finally to Scotland and to Stanley Junction, where the Highland Line used to part company with the Caledonian racetrack to Aberdeen via Forfar. It's Sunday morning, 9 July 1961, and Alan and I have just brought the car on the Motorail from King's Cross to Perth. I persuaded the sleeping car attendant to provide us with early morning tea while passing through Glen Farg, and we had breakfast in the Station Hotel. Now a holiday in the Highlands is before us, and to start we drove the few miles north of Perth and he photographed the Glasgow-Inverness, which had taken on a diner (the second vehicle) at Perth.

Doublebois, Cornwall: Class 42 No D819 *Goliath*, 9.5 am Swansea (High Street)-Penzance, 8 July 1960.
When the cities of Leicester, Nottingham and Sheffield got fidgety about the lack of HSTs on the Midland route, they pointed to the number running to Penzance and enquired at what speed they were obliged to run in the area of Doublebois. Here, as in much of Cornwall, the line twists and turns with numerous speed restrictions, and HSTs cannot show their paces. As a result of the lobbying many of the units were transferred from Paddington to St Pancras. Doublebois station closed in 1964. *2097*

Bishops Nympton & Molland, Devon; Class 22 No D6336, special train for filming by The Beatles, 6 March 1964.
The nearer sign on the left warns the drivers of goods trains to stop and pin down brakes in readiness for the descent towards South Molton from the outcrop of Exmoor. It's amazing to realise that over 100 years into the railway age, fully braked vacuum-fitted goods trains were still in the future. Although this route from Taunton was the shortest to North Devon (and the new road that has superseded it proves that), it was busy only on summer Saturdays and closed in 1966, since when passengers have been obliged to go via Exeter to Barnstaple. The headcode '1Z48' indicates a special train; The Beatles are on board. 3079

Watton-at-Stone, Hertfordshire; Class 40 No D206, 12.45 pm King's Cross-Leeds, 12 March 1961.
I talk about this place in the introductory text. 2389

Williton, Somerset; Class 119, 10.25 am Minehead-Paddington and Taunton-Minehead, 13 June 1970. Now that there is a Class 35 diesel preserved at Williton, this scene could be reproduced today as the West Somerset Railway has restored the line and this loop following BR closure in 1971. Harry, Alan and I stayed overnight in Williton in 1960 and needed a taxi between station and town because of the distance involved. 3692

Above Bruton, Somerset; Class 52, 9.30 am Plymouth-Paddington, 28 March 1965.

This is one of those casual, unplanned pictures, which normally turn out so well. My friend Ian Cantlon and I had returned from Derby the previous evening to near Radstock and had the Sunday morning to spare before seeing a special on the Somerset & Dorset. Bruton station survives, served by Bristol/Weymouth trains as at its inception, but in this picture is still lit by gas and even retains its signal box. It is close to Brewham bank with its 1 in 81 and 1 in 98 inclines, and the rear of the train is climbing into the level section where the station is located. Main-line trains have run this way since the turn of the century. 3384

Below Ashperton, Hereford & Worcester; Class 35, 12.05 pm Hereford-Paddington, 31 October 1964.

With only six months to closure, this station looks very run-down, and the so-called Paddington express does not deign to call. The seat with its GWR symbol survives, but the signals have gone. Now the line from Ledbury to the outskirts of Hereford is a single track, but it is used by daily HSTs. 3339

Above Dunton Green, Kent; Class 33, London (Victoria)-Dover Boat Train, unknown date.
Below Paddock Wood, Kent; Class 24 No D5000, Charing Cross-Dover (Priory), unknown date.

Two pictures of diesel-hauled trains on the electrified Southern Region route that now carries EuroStar services. As the notice reads, at Dunton Green you could still change there for Westerham (until 1961); the branch diverges to the left with its own platform face, but today the M25 has obliterated its route. The branch from Paddock Wood to Hawkhurst closed in the same year, but the line to Maidstone West survived and has been electrified.

Note the arrangements so that drivers can see signals easily. At Dunton Green the signal arm is on a short post so as to be visible beneath the platform awning, while at Paddock Wood there is a banner repeater on the footbridge that obscures the main signal beyond. *AL1277/AL1074*

Above South Tottenham, Greater London; Class 16, westbound freight, 17 January 1959.
Below West Green, Greater London; Class 31 No D5669, 12.10 pm North Woolwich-Palace Gates, 8 December 1962.

Two views in North London, an area not much frequented by me in its own right, and notably in the winter when it was nice to be near home. On the January Saturday Alan and I had met up at Waterloo and travelled by train to Chingford, Highams Park, Hoe Street and South Tottenham, where we took pictures of a number of freight trains, some steam-hauled and adding to the murky mist that abounded. We visited Seven Sisters, Enfield Town and Enfield Chase before ending up at King's Cross. The December 1962 sortie, by car with Bob Kirkland, included Coombe Road, Birkbeck and Ravensbourne. My diary records a picture at Oxted, but I cannot see how that fits in! *AL1055/2790*

Thorpe-by-Water, Leicestershire: Class 24 No D5077, 7.00 am Lowestoft Central-Birmingham (New Street), 1 September 1962.
Today a traveller west from Peterborough is obliged to take the former Midland route via Melton Mowbray and Leicester to Birmingham. The London & North Western provided an alternative via Rugby, first from Luffenham to Seaton, then direct from Peterborough, but this shut down in 1966. I am sorry, for the valley of the Welland is very pretty and looked nice from the carriage window. This view near Thorpe-by-Water is typical. Seaton, junction also for Uppingham, used to be busy in the early hours of the morning, when post was delivered there for all parts of Rutland. 2745

Above Hope, Derbyshire; Class 31 No D5850, 9.55 am Chinley-Sheffield (Midland), 16 May 1966.

When Beeching published his more positive report *The Development of the Major Trunk Routes* in 1965, he advocated the improvement of the Woodhead line between Sheffield and Manchester and the downgrading of the Hope Valley line. We know what management and lobbying devised – an Eastern Region stopping service cut back at New Mills (of all places) and London Midland through expresses with closure of Woodhead. The quarries at Hope and reduction in coal production have to be taken into account too. The trains are very important to hikers. 3570

Below Cowton Moor, North Yorkshire; Class 55, King's Cross-Edinburgh, 12 April 1965.

This is the only 'Deltic' in this book – what a disgrace! – seen on the East Coast Main Line (ECML) where the road to Richmond passes across. The local lines (newly ballasted) have since been lifted and the cutting looks much narrower now that nature has taken over. Overhead power lines for the electric trains have also been added. AL

Left Redmarshall, Cleveland; Class 25, eastbound freight, 12 April 1965.
The line from Ferryhill on the ECML to Norton Junction near Stockton-on-Tees survives, but for freight only; main-line diversions are a thing of the past since electrification. From here a line went north to Sunderland. *AL*

Below left Stanley Junction, Tayside; two Class 25s, 7.35 am Glasgow (Buchanan Street)-Inverness, 9 July 1961.
Alan and I have just brought the car off the sleeper service from King's Cross to Perth and we are looking forward to a fortnight in the Highlands. It's Sunday morning and few folk are abroad yet. Little did I think then that the Caledonian main line to Aberdeen (controlled by the other signal) would be subject to closure six years later when the service was diverted by Dundee. *AL1330*

Below Near Drumlithie, Grampian; two Class 21s, 1.5 pm Aberdeen-Edinburgh (Waverley), 28 May 1966.
These locos proved to be notoriously unreliable and went about in pairs. Because of high ground south of Stonehaven the ECML loops inland through Carmont and the train is about to regain contact with the main road to the south. *3599*

3.
ONE COACH TRAINS

In the previous volume of *Dawn of the Diesels* we looked at experiments in Buckinghamshire with single-unit railcars built mainly for branch line use. Not that these were new to the railway. They had been pioneered by the Great Western and built in the 1930s by AEC at Southall adjacent to the Uxbridge Road where it is crossed by the GWR main line on a skew bridge. Most of my pictures show units built in the 1940s. These were a natural development from the Sentinel railcars and other small steam units deemed adequate for local services.

Politicians have always dreamed of a bus on rails that could be manufactured cheaply in common with its road counterpart, and several attempts have been made, notably the vehicle that ran between Ipswich and Lowestoft in the 1980s, but without lasting success. The nearest innovation is the 'Pacer', and that is hardly the acme of comfort; its riding qualities have gained little from a century of rail travel. I remember travelling on a press run with the prototype from Leeds in 1981. At Ilkley, Peter Keen, Chief Commercial Manager at BR, whose parents had started my WEA class at Surbiton, mounted his soapbox to proclaim the train a great success. I couldn't help but share my reservations with him and he advised me that it would be excellent on welded rail. I often wonder, when travelling between Carnforth and Settle Junction, where welded rail is the exception, whether this message ever reached the operating people.

BR's demand for railbuses in their Modernisation Plan, backed by Government money, was such that many manufacturers were involved simultaneously. Of these I have managed to illustrate those built by AC Cars Ltd (of Thames Ditton near my former home), British United Traction (in Volume 1), Gloucester Railway Carriage & Wagon Co and Park Royal Vehicles Ltd. BR even went to the Germans – Waggon und Maschinenbau – and some of theirs are shown too; many survive on preserved lines.

Of the pictures of the Great Western railcars, three are taken between Bewdley and Tenbury Wells on visits with the late Bob Kirkland, who I still greatly miss and who was

such a good influence on my transport education, and his wife Phyl. We called at Newnham Bridge on our way back from Bantry in southern Ireland. Bob had heard (and even local people didn't know) that the passenger service from Cork was to cease at the end of March 1961. So with but a few days to spare we planned an itinerary using my Morris Minor to and from Fishguard, the boat to Rosslare and back for sleeping, and trains in Eire (John Faulkner, who was later to marry Phyl, joined us on the boat). We left on the Thursday and returned home on the Monday.

I have decided not to put Irish trains in this book, but of that trip I particularly remember the 4.10 pm Neath to Brecon – then the only train of the day – which stopped near Cray after being photographed so that the driver could satisfy himself that we had obtained a reasonable picture; the 63-bedroomed Abernant Lake Hotel where we were the only guests and were treated like royalty, my car looking quite forlorn by itself outside; the crossing of Cardigan branch trains at 7.7 pm at Llanglydwen in the light of the oil lamps; the helpful attendant at Fishguard who, on hearing we were returning the following night, told us to leave the car by the railings adjacent to the quay; the Great Southern & Western dining car with its clerestory roof and end table seating five on which we took breakfast westbound through Waterford direct to Mallow (and I thought the many spans of the viaduct over the River Barrow would never end) and dinner on returning from Cork, when emigrants joined the train at every wayside station; and the manure on the streets of Cork, and the old-fashioned buses there with luggage strung across the back. What happy days they were! The railcar at Newnham Bridge was the icing on the cake.

The picture at Maiden Newton reminds me of the day – 13 July 1957 – when Alan Wilson and I walked the branch from Toller Porcorum ('Of the pigs'!) to Powerstock over Wytherstone summit, with track permits supplied by the Southern Region, which had taken over this former Great Western branch following nationalisation. This was in preparation for an article to mark the Bridport centenary, which appeared in *The Railway Magazine* the subsequent November. This summit proved too much for a special organised by The Locomotive Club of Great Britain when returning from Bridport on 22 January 1967. The two tank engines had to await assistance by diesel loco D6541 summoned from Yeovil (I believe). I had travelled by car to photograph the train and was given sustenance from the dining car by Harry out of the train window near the summit. I then had to ring his very elderly mother to allay anxiety about his

late return and so avoid a potential call by her to the local police.

Bartlow was an unusual station, conventional platforms existing by the up and down lines to Cambridge and Colchester and a separate platform at right angles to these and some distance away along a footpath serving the train from Audley End. The station closed finally in 1967 and is now an example of a superb conversion, which I visited with a party from one of my weekend schools at Madingley Hall, Cambridge, in 1994.

Hythe End, Staines, Surrey; Great Western railcar No W21W, 6.12 pm Staines West-West Drayton, 22 July 1957.
Every picture tells a story, so they say, and this one shows opportunities lost. Under 19th-century 'privatisation' both the London & South Western and the Great Western served Staines and, as the picture shows, the railcar is divorced from the line below to Windsor & Eton Riverside. During the Second World War a connecting spur was put in

beyond this bridge to enable trains to run in an emergency from West Drayton to Staines Central. There are stabling sidings there and no reason, other than a BR regional boundary, why the Western trains should not connect with the Southern. Proposals were drafted but in the event the spur was lifted, Staines West closed with the passenger service on 29 March 1965 and the M25 was built on the route northwards. *1051*

Bewdley, Hereford & Worcester; Class 116 and Great Western railcar, 5.48 pm from Kidderminster and 4.20 pm Shrewsbury-Hartlebury, 5 May 1958. The old and the new come together. I'm glad to alight from the railcar (in red and cream livery) as it had become incredibly stuffy and noisy. Alan and I are on a circular tour from Hereford and have taken in Three Cocks Junction, Moat Lane Junction and Shrewsbury before reaching Bewdley. The final route was through Tenbury Wells using the steam train seen in platform 1. The station nameboard and the lamp tablets are of Great Western origin; it closed to BR traffic on 5 January 1970. *AL544*

Arley, Hereford & Worcester; Great Western railcar No W32W, 4.20 pm Shrewsbury-Kidderminster, 22 October 1960. This station has assumed fame in the BBC TV series *Oh, Dr Beeching!*. I had hoped to take my Morris Minor across the river at the end of Station Road, but the ferryman declined due to clearance problems. The vintage cars that it could accommodate must have declined in number, as a footbridge suffices today. The railcar is in BR green. 2287

Above Mortimer, Berkshire; Great Western parcels car No W34W, Reading (General)-Basingstoke, unknown date.

In this case company identities were altered following nationalisation. The railcar reminds us that the line from Reading to Basingstoke was originally Great Western, but when the Southern Region took over trains were extended to such places as Portsmouth, although these have since been cut back again following electrification in the Solent area. Through traffic from the North of England to the South Coast has been concentrated here since closure of the parallel routes. This railcar was one of only two built by the Great Western to carry parcels and was mainly employed conveying the products of J. Lyons, the confectioners, from Park Royal. *AL16*

Left Newnham Bridge, Hereford & Worcester; Great Western railcar, 11.00 am Kidderminster-Woofferton, 27 March 1961.
Above Neen Sollars, Hereford & Worcester; Great Western railcar No W23W, 11.00 am Kidderminster-Woofferton, 22 October 1960.
Right Wyre Forest, Hereford & Worcester; Great Western railcar No W23W, 9.50 am Tenbury Wells-Kidderminster, 22 October 1960.

These three pictures illustrate the cross-country route that linked Bewdley on the Severn Valley line with Woofferton on the Shrewsbury/Hereford line, and became Great Western/London & North Western Joint west of Tenbury Wells. Until closure in 1962 the timetable continued to recognise that distinction, although it was of no relevance to the passenger. Trains originating at Tenbury Wells went to Leominster and Ludlow. The equivalent main road parts company with the railway at Newnham Bridge to go over the hills. The railcars are painted in BR green livery. *2361/2291/2288*

Hermitage, Berkshire; Class 121, 3.36 pm Didcot-Newbury, 31 March 1962.
By the time this picture was taken, the Didcot, Newbury & Southampton Railway had been closed to passengers at the southern end and railcars like this were the order of the day. *2606*

Churn Halt, Berkshire (later Oxfordshire); Class 121, 3.36 pm Didcot-Newbury, 28 April 1962.
Churn Halt was built in 1888 for the competitions of the National Rifle Association, and was in an isolated part of the hills well away from any metalled road. I drove as near to it as I could and persuaded the then Station Master of Reading Southern, Bill Potter, and his wife to flag down the train and travel south to Compton where I would pick them up again. In the event the train sailed right through, but the driver braked, reversed the unit into the platform and they got on board. I've always understood that before the Second World War it was possible to stop a train here and go to Newcastle. Trains called only during daylight hours. *C1661*

Clevedon, Avon; Class 121, 2.17 pm to Yatton, 10 October 1960.
The Clevedon branch was significant in the battle between positive railwaymen and those anxious to please their political masters in the Beeching era. Gerard Fiennes was GM of the Western at the time and advocated retention of the branch, since direct costs did not greatly exceed direct revenue and contributory revenue was comparatively large. But (according to T. R. Gourvish in *British Railways 1948-73*, page 448) this argument cut no ice at HQ where Fred Margetts, respected by railwaymen and Beeching – who needed his expertise and standing in the railway family where he was an outsider – condemned Yatton-Clevedon as a 'bus service on rails' in a memo written on 17 December 1964, and stressed that 'arguments based on loss of contributory revenue should not prevail'. In this way was our fine railway network gradually destroyed. This branch closed on 3 October 1966. *2259*

Maiden Newton, Dorset; Class 121, 11.30 am Maiden Newton-Bridport, 1 September 1964.
The home signal guards the approach to the junction of the branch with the line from Castle Cary to Dorchester and Weymouth. In steam days the engine used to release itself from the bay platform by propelling its coaches up a slight incline and moving aside while they fly-shunted themselves back into the bay. Connections were made here for expresses to Paddington, but soon after nationalisation these were withdrawn and Weymouth was connected regularly with Waterloo, this route linking the coast with Bristol. 3310

Suckley, Hereford & Worcester; Class 121, 1.56 pm Bromyard-Worcester (Shrub Hill), 4 April 1964.

Although Suckley looks complete with its passing loop, in fact all signals have been removed and effectively the branch to Bromyard is a single line from its junction with the Worcester-Malvern route at Bransford Road. Until 1952 trains ran this way to Leominster on the Hereford-Shrewsbury line and connected there to Kington. The whole branch closed in 1964. *3119*

Above Wickham Bishops, Essex; German railbus, 12.13 pm Maldon East-Witham, 12 October 1963.

Left Maldon East, Essex; German railbus, 11.47 am from Witham, 12 October 1963. The contrast between the massive awning at the terminus and the open platform at one of the two wayside stations could hardly be greater. Until the outbreak of the Second World War Maldon had two stations and was linked to Woodham Ferrers on the Southminster branch. Two branch lines diverged at Witham on the main line to Ipswich; Braintree has been electrified but Maldon closed in 1964. It is more direct to drive to Chelmsford and join a London train there (until congestion intervenes!). *3021/3020*

Above **Bartlow, Essex; German railbus, 11.36 am from Audley End, 11 October 1958.**
I love the tall signal here with its economy in bearing signals for both directions. A footpath links this platform with those for Cambridge and Colchester. When the GLC built a new town at Haverhill they promised that this train from Audley End would run through – and it did – for a while! After September 1964 it didn't appear again. *1434*

Below **Gatehead, Strathclyde; AC Cars railbus, 8.18 am Dalmellington-Kilmarnock, 23 May 1964.**
Alan and I were expecting a steam loco and one coach, but instead this unit by AC Cars appeared. We are on holiday mainly in Galloway and the Borders. Gatehead shut in 1969 but trains still pass through – now on a single track – from Kilmarnock to Ayr, and for a time the London/Stranraer sleeper came this way. *3186*

Dollar, Central; Park Royal railbus, 12.26 pm from Stirling, 30 May 1964.
Later that holiday we were at Dollar and, as you can see from the shunt signal, the railcar is going to rest in a siding. The route eastwards to Kinross has only another fortnight to run. It was a beautiful ride and a pity it is lost. 3225

4.
STATION ARCHITECTURE

Rather a grand title, perhaps, for what follows, but nevertheless it includes a wide range of styles in both town and country.

The station building with the large awning at Bramley in Hampshire is typical of many Great Western rebuilds at the turn of the century. The line gave the company access to Basingstoke and the Southern Region and has grown in importance over the years as described under the picture taken near Mortimer (page 34). On 7 September 1963 I spent a very happy afternoon in the signal box there, when Signalman Hunt was in charge, tape recording the many cross-country trains that passed that way, some with Bulleid 'Pacifics', others with Great Western 'Halls'. The speed of the expresses on jointed track, coupled with the ringing of bells, movements of signal levers and shutting and opening of gates make a happy harmony of sounds.

We could have placed the views of Southill and Piddington in the 'one-coach train' section, but we thought that the station architecture was of sufficient interest to stand on its own. Between Bedford and Hitchin the route used to be the Midland main line before the opening of St Pancras enabled trains to reach London without recourse to Great Northern metals and consequent delays.

The large booking hall of the superb building at Mundesley-on-Sea was being used as a table-tennis and billiard room when I took my photograph in 1964. The train service, which had formerly run north along the coast, was now just a shuttle through Paston & Knapton to and from North Walsham on the Norwich/Cromer route.

Latterly Alfreton on the Erewash Valley route from St Pancras through Nottingham to Sheffield became one of the first 'park and ride' stations – for Mansfield – and

opened in a blaze of publicity. It has no resemblance to the typically Midland Railway station in the picture, and now that Mansfield has been reconnected to the passenger network its future may not be so upbeat.

When Alan and I arrived at Guisborough in 1960 our Circular Tour Tickets (for a fortnight's travel) allowed us to continue to Loftus, but the service had been cut back the previous week. It was so sparse that the next morning we had to use the bus to Nunthorpe to regain the rail network. The station building was full of cobwebs and had an air of total neglect. The town is now connected by a dual-carriageway road to Teesside to cope with demand, and it is difficult to see why the train service could not have been improved. Most of the route is still used by the service to Whitby. Guisborough closed to passengers on 2 March 1964.

One of our journeys to Alston was mentioned in the first chapter, and further pictures of the station appear elsewhere in the book. It is now the terminus of a miniature steam railway, BR closure having taken place in 1976. The overall roof has gone.

When I visited the Penrith/Keswick line by car in 1964 train working between Threlkeld and Penruddock was peculiar. Whereas the daily service of DMUs used both tracks in the conventional manner, the Saturday extras with their steam engines were restricted to the down line in both directions because of a weak bridge.

Large urban terminals such as those illustrated at Birkenhead (Woodside), Glasgow (St Enoch) and Dundee (West) are vulnerable to so-called progress as their huge sites are worth so much more to BR as supermarkets and the like. Thus all three have disappeared. That must be the point at which to conclude this chapter!

Bramley, Hampshire; Class 117, 4.40 pm Basingstoke-Reading, 27 June 1964.
I spent the Saturday afternoon at Mortimer and Bramley watching the 'Pines Express' go by amongst other trains; although the S&DR was still open, its most famous express had already been re-routed. Bramley has the classic Great Western station of the turn of the century together with signal box and gated level crossing. The DMU's rear blind is ready for coming back (or is it?). *3267*

Palace Gates, Greater London; Class 31 No D5654, 12.40 pm North Woolwich-Palace Gates, 8 December 1962.
Here's another picture on that cold December day when I had visited West Green (page 25) with Bob Kirkland. *2792*

Southill, Bedfordshire; Park Royal railbus, 11.52 pm Hitchin-Bedford (Midland), 8 August 1959.
This was a day devoted to the Midland between Hitchin and Bedford and Northampton, using VPA 312, my Morris Minor. The old signal at the platform end betrays its parentage, and it looks as though the wire could be tightened to advantage. Someone's returning from shopping in Hitchin, but not for much longer – closure took effect in 1962. 1761

Piddington, Northamptonshire; Park Royal railbus, 12.22 pm Northampton (Castle)-Bedford (Midland), 17 July 1959. I wonder if it's the same unit as that seen at Southill. The original ornate station, built to satisfy a nearby estate owner, has given way to something rather more austere yet quite attractive. It was very remote and was retained as a siding to an MoD establishment long after closure to passengers in 1962. I always enjoyed visiting these wayside stations, driving up their overgrown drives and standing on the platforms as nature picked away at them. On this occasion I'm with Geoff Hunt and we are going by road to Melton Mowbray via Kelmarsh and Marefield Junction, coming back via Lowesby Tunnel, Wing and Lutterworth. *1732*

Above Mundesley-on-Sea, Norfolk; Metro-Cammell 'Lightweight', 7.37 pm to Norwich (Thorpe), 8 August 1964.

Right Paston & Knapton, Norfolk; Metro-Cammell 'Lightweight', 6.7 pm Mundesley-on-Sea-North Walsham, 8 August 1964.
It was a lovely sunny evening when I drove to Paston & Knapton and Mundesley-on-Sea to watch the train go to North Walsham and back again. The resort was given the treatment with a splendid station with clock tower and weather-vane. The 40 mph sign at Paston gives warning of the condition of the track, which became disused, as so often, in 1964. *3291/3290*

Alfreton, Derbyshire; Class 108, 2.33 pm Sheffield (Midland)-Nottingham (Midland), 2 March 1962.

Accountancy seems to demand that expenditure be handled in separate compartments. Hence although trains can carry passengers and freight on the same journey, this seems to be discouraged. I hope a change will be forthcoming. At Alfreton, on a snowy March day, there are plenty of parcels for the guard's van of the DMU. Look at all the trucks in the sidings! *2581*

Birkenhead (Woodside), Merseyside; Class 108, to Chester, 27 April 1963.
This gloomy place encapsulates what a railway station was like to so many people. It was eventually to close, but not for another four years, and goodness knows what it felt like then. It has since been swept away. The porter is trying desperately to clean the platform; the woman is in earnest conversation with the inspector. Not much going on, really. *2862/2863*

Left   Guisborough, Cleveland; Class 114, 6.56 pm to Middlesbrough, 23 May 1960.
I have written about Guisborough and its railway at some length in the introductory text, so will leave it at that. *1950*

Below left Richmond, North Yorkshire; Class 101, to Darlington, 12 April 1965.
This handsome terminus has been preserved as a garden centre and the surroundings have become a municipal country park complete with signal box. A pleasant walk uses the trackbed and this seems as good a use as any when the trains have gone. The bridge carrying the road from the town over the Swale is still owned by BR as the County Council declines to take it over; it carries a North Eastern Railway bridge plate. *AL*

Below Alston, Cumbria; Class 101, 12.45 pm to Haltwhistle, 2 June 1960.
Although Alston features elsewhere, its station deserves a place here complete with soot marks where the engine stood before the coming of the DMUs. The buffer-stops seem a bit weak; obviously some rationalisation has been undertaken with the removal of a turntable, but a limited future doesn't justify much expenditure. *2045*

Above left Keswick, Cumbria; Derby 'Lightweight', 12.25 pm Workington (Main)-Carlisle, 15 August 1964.

Keswick station was a real tribute to this Lakeside town. The adjoining hotel and the carriage drive to the main street give it a touch of class so often missing elsewhere. Sad that the Wilson Government saw the development of West Cumbria and the improvement of the A66 beside Bassenthwaite Lake as incompatible with the railway that went under the road. From the Penrith direction Keswick held out until 1972, but the end was by then inevitable. *3300*

Left Threlkeld, Cumbria; Derby 'Lightweight', 12.40 pm Keswick-Penrith, 15 August 1964.

This station closed the same day. Set amidst magnificent country it in no way clashed with the landscape and was somewhat unusual in having an island platform. At the end steam trains had to set back and use the 'wrong' line to the east. *3299*

Top Hamilton Central, Strathclyde; Class 101, 4.15 pm Hamilton Central-Coalburn, 20 May 1964.

I have very few pictures of stations in the Glasgow conurbation, so this one is of particular interest. We are about to join this train to travel to Coalburn and return to Stonehouse empty stock (see page 79). Obviously the through lines have been lifted; I wonder if the overall roof was originally glazed. *3171*

Above Dundee West, Tayside; Class 101, 10.50 am to Perth, 19 May 1964.

Dundee West deserved to close. The competitive nature of this ex-Caledonian terminus was displayed in its vast St Pancras-like structure, and it saw its last train in May 1965. It has since been razed to the ground in favour of a road network for the Tay Bridge; the station of that name is submerged nearby. The barrow in the foreground bears witness to the attempt at keeping the platforms clean. *3159*

Glasgow (St Enoch), Strathclyde; Class 45, 'Thames-Clyde Express' to London (St Pancras), 30 March 1964.
Certainly St Enoch remained glazed until the end (1966), but has since disappeared. The 'Thames Clyde Express' waits to leave for St Pancras via the Glasgow & South Western and Settle & Carlisle lines. It's Easter Monday and I'm expecting to travel behind *Glen Douglas* via Bathgate to Edinburgh, then to Alloa, Denny and eventually to Buchanan Street. I slipped on a moist sleeper at Denny, which acted as a caution for the future. *3107*

5.
BRANCH LINE TERMINI

The terminus at Severn Beach is a little unusual. Today all the trains from Bristol turn back there and at some times of day they are even replaced by buses. It is one of the city's few suburban services. But when the branch was extended from Avonmouth in 1900 the trains sometimes continued to Pilning (closed in 1964) on the South Wales main line, and a number returned to Temple Meads by way of Patchway. Alan and I visited it during a railtour from Paddington, which also took in Clevedon (page 37), the Yatton-Wells-Witham route and the Wylye Valley line to Salisbury. Pilning was the railhead for the car service through the Severn Tunnel.

There were three branch line termini in the Tendring Hundred in Essex. My pictures of Brightlingsea show the one that closed in June 1964. The others are served by electric trains, which were newly introduced from Colchester only when we made our visit in May 1959. Having returned in the DMU to Wivenhoe (where passengers often had to change, which on such a short journey did not encourage patronage), we turned east to Walton-on-the-Naze, took a bus to Clacton and came home from there. Those two branches diverge at Thorpe-le-Soken. Since electrification the area has built up a substantial commuter traffic to London.

Perhaps Aldeburgh, further up the coast and home to Gerard Fiennes and the composer Benjamin Britten, who put it more on the map, was unlucky in losing its branch line in 1966. Had it been a seaside resort like Skegness it might have survived. Mrs Barbara Castle, then Minister of Transport, had a soft spot for such places, no doubt recalling their importance in Wakes Weeks in Lancashire in days gone by. Her officials gave a clue as to the political tactics involved when they admitted that two proposals in East Anglia – Saxmundham-Aldeburgh and the East Suffolk Line – would make useful refusals to balance "awkward consents" such as the Great Central (Gourvish, *British Railways 1948-73*, page 447). Although Fiennes proved the case for 'basic railway operation' for the East Suffolk Line, and this was agreed by the Minister, it was

more than 15 years before the money was made available by BR.

Still further up the coast, Wells-next-the-Sea had been the terminus of two branches. A train to Norwich via the branch from Dereham and Wymondham is illustrated. The other route via Burnham Market, closed to passengers in 1952, gave access to Heacham and the line from Hunstanton to King's Lynn.

Yet further up the coast is Hornsea, which retained its train service until 1964. Like Withernsea (page 13) it was the seaside lung for Hull to which even the humblest could afford to make their way on Bank Holidays and the like. The branch had the misfortune to include a station known as Swine, after the village nearby!

A terminus on the coast that has survived is Whitby, although but a shadow of its former self. Today a handful of trains continue to arrive from Middlesbrough via Battersby anchored to a contract from North Yorkshire County Council to convey children to and from school. The road on Limber Hill at Glaisdale is too steep to be safe for coaches on a regular basis, especially in winter weather. If money is found to improve the road, the future of the railway will be in danger again. Meanwhile such bodies as The Esk Valley Rail Partnership, bringing together local authorities and other parties interested in the railway, are working to develop a tourism package similar to that on the Settle & Carlisle, and this focus can only be to the good. Hitherto Whitby had been host to trains from Teesside via Loftus, from Scarborough (in which Borough Whitby now finds itself) and from Malton (and hence York). This latter route now forms the North Yorkshire Moors Railway from Pickering and there has been much talk about extending its services over public metals to Whitby, but there are a number of elderly bridges over the Esk to bear in mind.

The other terminals illustrated are all inland. Clayton West was one that I never thought would survive until 1983. The branch was intended to continue to Barnsley, but never got beyond this village. Only the good service

of DMUs from Huddersfield (and beyond) enabled it to continue so long.

We have 'gone to town' on Alston because the old buildings are such distinctive relics of the old railway age, besmirched with soot yet home to DMUs. The pictures may help modellers! BR were determined to close this line. Precision Products, a local firm, always sent its goods by train; this revenue must have upset the closure ledgers, so facilities to carry goods were withdrawn. Because of the nature of the valley roads it was impossible to substitute a bus service without the construction of a new road and bridge over the river at Coanwood, so this was duly done. It is an irony that the fine viaduct at Lambley, which needed significant maintenance to continue to support a train service, is now being renovated with grants under other legislation; perhaps this is merely a facelift!

Opposite **Brightlingsea, Essex; Class 105, 1.03 pm to Wivenhoe, 3 May 1959.**
In the upper photograph Harry is reviewing the situation in his inimitable style and is wondering why no lunch has been available. I think that he had to wait until the evening for his main meal. In the second picture Alan has joined him on the seat and an alfresco lunch is in progress. *1596/1597*

The branch to Cheadle in Staffordshire also has a distinctive feature apart from the absurd need to change sometimes at Cresswell on the short journey to Stoke-on-Trent. Originally the line passed through a tunnel; this became unsafe in 1918 and was patched up, but eventually the track was re-routed round the circumference of the hill in 1933. So simple, yet had it been the Beeching era the condition of the tunnel would have been paraded as an excuse for closure. In fact, Beeching won in any case and the last trains ran in 1963.

I have memories of Cresswell. I stopped one of my Inspection Saloon trips (see Volume 1) there for photographs and it's the only occasion when someone was left behind. Fortunately he was able to board a service train and catch us up at Derby before we ventured to Wirksworth!

Below **Severn Beach, Avon; Class 116, 1.00 pm Severn Beach-Bristol (Temple Meads), 10 October 1960.**
The train on the left has come from Bristol and has terminated in the bay. The train on the right will continue to Bristol via Pilning and the main line. *2255*

Aldeburgh, Suffolk; Metro-Cammell 'Lightweight', 12.18 pm to Ipswich, 13 July 1963.
This print might have been shown under 'Station Architecture' because of its overall roof. The previous station, Thorpeness, was also distinctive in having waiting accommodation comprised of two Great Eastern railway coaches. From Saxmundham the track is retained today to Sizewell Nuclear Power Station. *2909*

Wells-next-the-Sea, Norfolk; Derby 'Lightweight', 2.9 pm to Norwich, 1 August 1960. Behind the station wall is the closed engine shed. We have come from Liverpool Street via Norwich with breakfast on 'The Norfolkman', will return to Dereham, and will then head for Swaffham and Thetford. We shall return home via the Ely North Curve and Peterborough with dinner on the train to King's Cross. 2138

Above **Hornsea, Humberside; Class 105, from Hull, 3 August 1964.**
Another overall roof, and a seat with supports representing serpents. On the left are two excursion platforms. *3285*

Left **Cheadle, Staffordshire; Class 104, 5.40 pm to Stoke-on-Trent, 6 May 1961.**
I spent the weekend at Hoar Cross while exploring railways in Staffordshire with Bob Kirkland. We also visited Burton, Alton Towers, Caldon Low, Alsop-en-le-Dale, Leigh, Tutbury and Uttoxeter. *2403*

Clayton West, West Yorkshire; Class 101, 1.00 pm to Bradford (Exchange), 11 July 1964.
I took one of my nephews with me on this occasion in the hope of encouraging an interest in trains – but to no avail! Probably a wait of 90 minutes for a late-running service at Bamford had something to do with his lack of interest! The station building survives today as part of the narrow-gauge Kirklees Light Railway. 3275

Above Whitby Town, North Yorkshire; Class 101, 4.25 pm Scarborough-Middlesbrough, 23 May 1960.
This illustrates the period of transition from steam to diesel; the DMU is on the Scarborough/Middlesbrough service and the steam is due to go to Malton. *AL1079*

Below Middleton-in-Teesdale, County Durham; Class 101, 10.00 am to Darlington, 4 June 1960.
Here the lady porter took great interest in horticulture. There was a fine flower bed at the station entrance and climbing plants in the Booking Hall. We came in from Bishop Auckland and walked to our hotel, but Harry insisted on a taxi back in the morning! 2050

Richmond, North Yorkshire; Class 114, to Darlington, 13 April 1965.
The goods train in the picture is headed by Class 'K1' 2-6-0 No 62041, and followed the passenger to Darlington. To reach the town square from the station involves a crossing of the river and a climb up a steep hill. Perhaps that's why the road vehicle triumphed. 3399

Alston, Cumbria; Class 101, to Newcastle (*above*), to Haltwhistle (*opposite page*), 2 June 1960.
The overall roof and the engine shed were demolished before the station closed. It's now the terminus of The South Tynedale Railway, a narrow-gauge steam system. *AL1076/2043/2044*

Left **Silloth, Cumbria; Derby 'Lightweight', 10.10 am to Carlisle, 25 May 1959.**
A Scottish Railway in England! The branch was operated by the North British and closed on 7 September 1964. We later travelled from Carlisle to Newcastle and picked up a BBC tape recorder at Manors before staying overnight in Morpeth. Next day we went on the goods along the Wansbeck Valley. *1629*

Below left **Largs, Strathclyde; two Class 107s, 4.35 pm to Glasgow (St Enoch), 23 May 1964.**
Alan and I are having our annual holiday in Scotland and have come here from Kilmarnock. We continue north by bus to the train at Wemyss Bay. Almost 20 years later I was to bring the Saloons here en route from Alnmouth, via Cardenden, to Stranraer, and we were delayed near Paisley after running over a mattress thrown on the track. *3187*

Below **Lanark, Strathclyde; Class 107, 5.7 pm from Glasgow (Central), 21 May 1964.**
We have left the car at Muirkirk and taken the goods train to Mauchline, then passenger services via Glasgow to Edinburgh and a through steam train from there to Lanark via Carstairs and the Silvermuir Junction east-to-south curve – our steam engine is in the picture. After dinner we took the DMU to Muirkirk and retrieved the car. *3178*

6.
SIGNALS AND SIGNAL BOXES

et's look first at the junctions illustrated, as they all have a story to tell. Southcote Junction marks the divergence of what was originally the two lines of the Berks & Hants Railway, south to Basingstoke and west to Devizes. As it also used to mark the boundary between the Southern and Western Regions I needed two track permits to take my pictures. My reason for the visit in October 1964 was anticipation that the Newcastle-Bournemouth train would be discontinued – certainly steam would disappear – and here was an important junction on its route that I would like to record for my collection. It came to time behind a nice clean 'Hall' and was duly bagged!

About half-an-hour later this train would reach Worting Junction, our next illustration, where the Southern routes from Waterloo to Bournemouth and to the West Country part company. It was a tradition for some years that Harry, Alan and myself foregathered there on the Saturday afternoon prior to a Bank Holiday to watch the endless procession of trains, many with northern destinations or origins, come and go. On one occasion Her Majesty the Queen came by en route to Portsmouth to board the Royal Yacht for the Isle of Wight and Cowes Week. We always ended the visit with dinner at The Red Lion in Basingstoke.

Wellington No 1 signal box marked the western end of the only significant line that I am conscious was built by a railway *and* canal company, the Shropshire Union. Trains set out from Stafford on the West Coast Main Line and often continued to Shrewsbury. Passenger trains were withdrawn in 1964 but the Wellington end was retained for military traffic as far as Donnington until comparatively recently.

Ledbury Tunnel Junction was unusual in that it was necessitated by a single-bore tunnel on a double-track section from Colwall, the line doubling again in Ledbury station at the other end. The junction was abolished when the route was made single track throughout from Malvern Wells to Ledbury.

There is a considerable disparity of speed between the electric expresses and the 'Sprinter' units setting out north from Grantham station, through Peascliffe Tunnel, to reach the Barkston Junctions and regain their own line. As a result, more than seasonal trains are now tending to use the Allington/Barkston section. The signalman can reach the box at Barkston East Junction only by driving down the edge of a field – the farmer has erected a 40 mph road sign presumably to discipline him on his way home!

Like Southcote, Culworth Junction, in itself a quite insignificant spot, is another key point on the network. Here trains bound for the South Coast (other than those to Ramsgate and Hastings, for instance) used to diverge from the Great Central main line to Marylebone and head west for the Cherwell Valley and the Great Western at Banbury. As signalling on the main line came to be rationalised during the run-down to closure, delays could peak here on a summer Saturday afternoon, particularly as Eydon Road survived close by but Chacombe Road was rarely opened, both located between Culworth and Banbury. I sometimes wondered whether the timetable compilers were aware of the situation. On the late afternoon of 13 August 1960 I saw trains held simultaneously by signals on each line at Culworth Junction due to congestion. Now there is nothing left.

The picture of Bicester North brings back memories of my recording for the BBC a journey on one of the last slip-coach workings on BR, namely the 5.10 pm Paddington-Wolverhampton (Low Level). This slipped the last coach when passing above the Oxford-Bletchley Line and it came to rest on the track being used by the Pullman in the photograph. In the adjacent platform was the 4.15 pm Paddington-Banbury stopping service. The engine from this was released to go forward and back on to the slip coach, which was then attached to the Banbury train when the passengers had alighted.

I made my first recording on Friday 13 May 1960. I'm not normally very superstitious, but. . . Everything went well with the interview at Paddington station and the guard was very affable and chatty during the journey, but, to my horror and acute embarrassment, when the actual slip took place the tape recorder failed to start. It proved to be a genuine electrical fault caused perhaps by the vibration of the coach. I made a second, successful, attempt the following Wednesday and the edited result was broadcast on 13 July 1960. I believe it may now be a unique recording.

Although the service illustrated in my picture was withdrawn in 1970, it is possible that Swavesey station may see trains again. One of the tracks remains in situ and the formation was not transferred to Railtrack as part of the changes in the rail industry in April 1994. It was subsequently managed by the British Rail Property Board, while Cambridgeshire County Council carried out a

feasibility study and aimed to submit a formal bid for funding to the Department of Transport in 1996.

I had better draw this chapter to a close. Before so doing may I draw your attention, please, to the height of the signal at Walsingham – what a magnificent piece of timber! Why was it necessary on a line with such slow trains? A comparison of the modern US Air Force base at Lakenheath and the vintage level crossing gates at the station, which the signalman has to come out and move by hand, must tell us something. I do not recall the DMU posing for our photographs at Alton Heights, but it must be so as we never went near there by road. The train took commuters home from Glasgow to Coalburn, then returned empty stock, with us on special permits, to Stonehouse. The driver/guard must have spoilt us. Those were the days!

Southcote Junction, Berkshire; Class 205, 3.53 pm Reading (General)-Basingstoke, 12 October 1964.
It's a Monday afternoon: I've been undertaking a test in the morning

and now I'm free to concentrate on the railway. Having seen the Newcastle-Bournemouth I hung around for a DMU to Basingstoke and another to Bedwyn so as to photograph both routes. *3330*

Worting Junction, Hampshire; Class 118, 12.06 pm Portsmouth & Southsea-Reading (General), 5 August 1961.
In addition to the DMU, which has come over Battledown Flyover, an up West of England express is appearing from underneath and they will race each other to Basingstoke station. The signal box has long since gone. 2505

Above Bicester North, Oxfordshire; 'Blue Pullman', Paddington-Birmingham (Snow Hill), 16 July 1965.
I describe happenings here in the text on page 68. When *Clun Castle* hauled the last scheduled steam train from Paddington – the 4.15 pm to Banbury on 11 June – it was looped here for the 'Blue Pullman' to overtake. *3479*

Right Wellington No 1 signal box, Shropshire; Class 116, 6.32 pm Wolverhampton (Low Level)-Shrewsbury, 16 May 1958.
Alan and I are staying at All Stretton in the first B&B I ever used on my own, back in 1956. According to my diary we have visited Presthope (for the goods to Longville-in-the-Dale on Wenlock Edge), and Ellesmere before arriving at Wellington. The signal box is of an unusual design, perhaps because from here to Shrewsbury the route is of London & North Western and Great Western Joint origin. *AL1057*

Ledbury Tunnel Junction, Hereford & Worcester; Class 119, 12.3 pm Birmingham (Snow Hill)–Carmarthen, 29 July 1962.
This train of nine coaches (unusually) is going from Birmingham to Cardiff via Stourbridge, Worcester and Hereford. 2721

Above Walsingham, Norfolk; Metro-Cammell 'Lightweight', 3.30 pm Wells-next-the-Sea-Norwich, 8 August 1964.
This line closed completely in October 1964, but the station has since become a church and the trackbed northwards is used by the Wells & Walsingham narrow-gauge steam railway. *3288*

Right Swavesey, Cambridgeshire; Class 105, 4.5 pm Cambridge-Wisbech, 23 March 1963.
Don't miss the nice Great Eastern lower-quadrant signal, which gives the train the right-away. Also the station is lit by electricity – quite unusual at this time – although the post for the oil lamp is still standing. *2850*

Below Lakenheath, Suffolk; Class 31 No D5564, 2.34 pm Norwich (Thorpe)-Peterborough (North), 14 February 1960.
There are gated crossings, hand-worked by the signalman, to this day, which must strike our American friends stationed nearby as extraordinary in the 1990s. I am on a day out by car visiting Elsenham, Bury, Thetford and Mildenhall. *1858*

Bottom Oundle, Northamptonshire; Class 31, 9.35 am Northampton (Castle)-Peterborough East, 20 April 1963.
I'm en route from King's Cliffe to Doncaster with David Lawrence. This line was promoted from Blisworth (on the West Coast Main Line) by the London & Birmingham Railway. It closed for normal passenger services in 1964, but was retained for goods from the north only until 1972. There's a nice old-fashioned gated level crossing with a London & North Western lower-quadrant signal. *2856*

Right Haven House, Lincolnshire; Class 31, ECS Skegness-Boston, 10 July 1965.
Haven House retained its somersault signals longer than many – on concrete posts made at Melton Constable. The gates are hand-operated. I moved on to Tetford for the night. *3477*

Below right North Thoresby, Lincolnshire; two Class 114s, 12.58 pm Grimsby Town-Peterborough North, 16 August 1969.
This is the East Lincs Line which carried expresses from Grimsby and Cleethorpes to King's Cross prior to closure in 1970. The trackbed is now a very straight main road between Boston and a point north of Spalding. The DMU was running on a section of line authorised for 'tail traffic' and there is a four-wheeled van bringing up the rear. *3666*

Barnetby, Humberside; Class 114, 12.16 pm Doncaster-Cleethorpes, 3 August 1959. There's a wonderful array of signals here, some of which have survived rationalisation. On one occasion – 20 September 1986 – we made a Newark/London connection here from the Inspection Saloon at 7.45 pm, and the Station Inspector, who had kindly turned out to make sure that the link was made, accepted a glass of sherry. The connection from London had been made at Newark at 10.05 before we travelled via Lowfield to Bottesford West Junction. We had to make sure that the comparatively slow-moving Saloon did not impede expresses on the East Coast Main Line. Hence we joined it at Shaftholme Junction right behind an HST and reached Newark just ahead of the next one before we turned off again.

1758

Right Culworth Junction, Northampton-shire; Class 37, 10.8 am York-Bournemouth West, 5 August 1965.
The train is composed of green coaches, so it has to be a Tuesday, Thursday or Saturday, as the Southern coaches ran north at the beginning of each week and returned each alternate day. I have no track permit but it seemed so important to reach this location, remote from any road, that I took a chance with the signalman and walked along the cess. He proved to be interested in my endeavour, far nicer than the bull I encountered while crossing the field to the line! *3490*

Below Eydon Road, Northamptonshire; Class 37 No D6813, 8.30 am Newcastle-Bournemouth, 25 July 1964.
Culworth was a Thursday, Eydon Road a Saturday, so it's a similar set of coaches. Due to the proximity of the two boxes compared with the distance (6 miles) from Eydon Road to Banbury Junction (Chacombe Road normally being switched out), the express has caught up its relief, steam-hauled, in front, and is crawling towards the starting signal, which remains obstinately at danger. *3282*

Left Commondale, North Yorkshire; Class 114, Middlesbrough-Scarborough, 2 May 1964.
We've actually come to a picture of a line still open to passengers – just! It is useful for the village to have a transport outlet to Teesside. *3150*

Below Featherstone Park, Northumberland; Class 101, Alston-Newcastle, 14 April 1965.
We're on the way by car from Wearhead to Armathwaite, and have stopped off here. Featherstone Park itself is just over the hill from the station. Notice the North Eastern Railway slotted-post lower-quadrant signal with its fine finial. *3404*

Above Penruddock, Cumbria; Derby 'Lightweight', 9.25 am Workington-Penrith, 15 August 1964.
By chance I am again on my way to Armathwaite, this time from the west rather than the east. Do observe the distinctive Cockermouth, Keswick & Penrith Railway signal box. *3296*

Below Alton Heights signal box, Strathclyde; Class 101, Coalburn-Stonehouse ECS, 20 May 1964.
Until the train drew up here I had never heard of Alton Heights signal box, and would have imagined it to be in Hampshire, perhaps. It had been the junction for a line east to Southfield Junction providing an alternative route between Coalburn and Hamilton. This appears to have been lifted recently and the post for the splitting signal for the branch has lost its arm. Such a big box was now handling hardly any traffic and closed on 4 October 1965. *AL1058*

7.
VIADUCTS AND BRIDGES

Below Saltash, Cornwall; two Class 22s, 5.30 am Paddington-Penzance, 9 July 1960.

It rained as I arrived here with Hugh Davies, and a lady (I hope) invited me into the upper room of her house so as to get a better picture. The piers of the new road bridge, then under construction, protrude into the view. At one time the bridge was the only piece of single track between Paddington and Penzance (rather like at Montrose on the East Coast Main Line). By crossing the Tamar the train is leaving Devon for Cornwall.

When the Britannia Bridge near Bangor caught fire some years ago there was talk of abandoning it and not reopening the railway to Holyhead. This caused apprehension in Cornwall where the Royal Albert Bridge is now the only one carrying a major railway into the Principality. It is 2,190 feet long, there are 17 approach spans and two main spans each of 445 feet in length. There is 100 feet clearance from water level at high tide. *2102*

Right Meldon Viaduct, Devon; Class 42 No D808 *Centaur*, 10.12 am Plymouth-Brighton, 2 July 1966.

This viaduct over the West Okement River on the main line to Plymouth closed in 1968 and is situated close to Meldon Quarry, from which BR draws some of its ballast. Despite the withdrawal of other Southern Region West Country expresses when the Western Region took over west of Wilton, this service survived and today turns south at Exeter to terminate at Paignton. The maximum height of the viaduct is 120 feet. *3614*

Below right Clifton Bridge, Avon; Class 116, 5.15 pm Portishead-Bristol (Temple Meads), 11 May 1963.

The bridge this time does not carry a railway, but like the Royal Albert Bridge was designed by Brunel. It spans the Avon Gorge near Bristol, through which runs the Portishead branch on the south side. Note the width between the tracks, which indicates broad gauge origin. The passenger service was withdrawn in 1964. *2878*

Knucklas, Powys; Class 37, Swansea (Victoria)-Shrewsbury, 17 July 1965.
This viaduct is 214 yards long, has crenellated parapets and castellated ends. It crosses a tributary of the River Teme made famous by Housman in his poetry and Butterworth and Vaughan Williams in their music. We had expected this train to be hauled by a 'Jubilee' steam locomotive and were disappointed as it came into sight. Now I am pleased, for it can be included in this book! 3481

Above **Whitby, Prospect Hill, North Yorkshire; Class 101, 6.52 pm Scarborough-Darlington.**
Below **Larpool Viaduct, Whitby, North Yorkshire, Class unknown, Scarborough-Whitby (Town), both 21 May 1960.**
Larpool Viaduct has lain idle since the last regular trains passed over it in 1965. To reach sea-level and the terminus at Whitby Town trains crossing the viaduct proceeded by West Cliffe station on the Saltburn line, reversed, and descended the sharp curve to Bog Hall Junction on the Esk Valley route from Grosmont. The viaduct is 915 feet long and 120 feet high. *1939/1941*

Above Deepdale Viaduct, County Durham; Class 101, 11.30 am
Darlington-Penrith, 28 May 1960.
I refer to this visit in the introduction to Chapter 1 (page 9). The
viaduct is 740 feet long with a maximum height of 161 feet. *1999*

Below Hownes Gill Viaduct, Durham; two Class 104s, Consett-
Waskerley RCTS Special, 10 April 1965.
By the time this view was taken special trains had to be formed of
DMUs as the weight of locomotives was forbidden on this slender
viaduct. Previously trains went this way from Consett to Bishop
Auckland via Wear Valley Junction. There is now a footpath across the
viaduct, which is a listed structure 730 feet long with a maximum
height of 150 feet. *3394*

Shankend Viaduct, Borders; Class 45, 9.15 am St Pancras-Edinburgh (Waverley) ('The Waverley'), 20 July 1963.
You can just see the remote station of Shankend to the south of the viaduct. 'The Waverley' express is made up entirely of BR Mark 1 stock in maroon and looks very handsome. 2938

Throsk, Central; Class 100, Larbert-Alloa, 30 May 1964.
This is the 'other' Forth Bridge, 1,614 feet long, and could be likened to the Kincardine road bridge in relation to the M90. Do note the control cabin mid-stream, which swung the bridge clear of shipping, and the 'pulpit' for exchange of the single-line token. *3224*

8.
RAILWAYMEN

The line from Welwyn Garden City to Leighton Buzzard had the misfortune to cross the natural commuter flow to London by the Midland, to be run in two sections, reflecting ownership prior to the 1920s (GNR/LNWR), and to link two regions of BR, the Eastern and the London Midland. As a result, despite some overlapping of trains between Luton (Bute Street) and Dunstable before closure of the western end in 1962, a through journey was well nigh impossible even though the complete route was barely 25 miles in length. The Eastern ran basically a peak-hour and Saturday service, which was discontinued in 1965.

When the Oxford-Cambridge direct service was threatened with closure, effective, constant and long-term opposition led to the retention of the section from Bletchley to Bedford and eventual routing of the trains into the Midland station. Had similar action been taken along the line the rest might well have been saved. As it was, 700 of the 1,300 written objections were on printed postcards provided by the NUR; these would be far less effective than even the briefest individual letter written in manuscript.

The route west of Bletchley is discussed in Volume 1; at one time there was official talk of a 'Sprinter' service this way from Swindon to Peterborough via Corby and Oakham, which could be very useful to me. As it is, the two pictures included here show stations closed in 1968. At Lord's Bridge there is the unique spectacle of radio telescopes along the trackbed.

But I've barely mentioned railwaymen yet!

The man at Ynys (where we are looking at the back of the train) works a ground frame to operate his signals. Despite more than 100 years of trains there, the authorities have not yet provided a shelter for the levers and he has to stand outside, often in the rain and cold. Closure took place in 1964. When the track was lifted the

contractors left the signals in situ, complete with semaphores to guard the green ride that remained!

It's time to change shift at Broom Junction and the signalman is on his way home by bike. It's a busy Whit Monday when the service on the Barnt Green-Evesham line was transformed to a train every 45 minutes, some returning quickly as empty stock to bring more trippers out of Birmingham. To see a DMU here was very rare indeed. The signals at danger control the Stratford-on-Avon & Midland Junction Railway route to Towcester. It seems incredible now to think that the Midland found it worthwhile to bring banana trains this way from Avonmouth to London via Bedford.

Using the goods train to come down Weardale (see Chapter 1) meant that we were in a position to take the 4.15 pm train from Bishop Auckland to Barnard Castle, the return working of the only passenger train of the day that way, providing for school children. The picture shows it in the bay at Barnard Castle forming the next service to Middleton-in-Teesdale, which we rejoined, with the crew relaxing on the seat as the connection from Darlington to Penrith comes to a stand. That evening we were to experience small-town cinema. The building resembled a private house and the auditorium was filled with an assortment of settees and armchairs. At the appointed time a lady came on the stage and asked if we were ready to begin. The projectionist then ran *I'm All Right, Jack* with Peter Sellers, which we thoroughly enjoyed.

No longer is there a station at Kilkerran, but the track layout survives as a loop on the single line from Dalrymple Junction, Ayr, to Girvan. I was driving casually over the hills from Newton Stewart when I realised that a train was due here and hurried on to see it – hence the picture and the porter looking for passengers. Sadly there were none.

Alton Heights signal box brings us back to where we were at the end of Chapter 6, and the kindly driver and guard. Perhaps that's where we should leave it.

Umberleigh, Devon; Class 35, 1.55 pm Ilfracombe-Paddington, 13 June 1970.
The signalman is about to deliver the tablet to the driver of the Ilfracombe-Paddington express for the single-line to Eggesford. *3694*

Above right **Ayot, Hertfordshire; Class 20, 1.15 pm Dunstable (North)-Hatfield, 26 June 1960.**
Ayot is synonymous with the name of George Bernard Shaw, a resident for more than 40 years. The station here closed in 1949 but the loop survived until the service was discontinued in 1965. It is a Great Northern signal box. *2074*

Right **Harpenden East, Hertfordshire; Class 20, 2.40 pm Dunstable (North)-Hatfield, 25 June 1960.**
I spent the day in the car securing pictures of the branch between Welwyn Garden City and Luton Hoo, particularly where the route passed under the Midland main line. Saturday was the day on which most trains were operated; it's quite surprising, however, to see a goods, especially as it is comprised of but one wagon. The electric lamps are of LNER style. *2078*

Left Willington, Bedfordshire; Class 108, 9.58 am Cambridge-Bletchley, 21 March 1962.

The signalman is bringing the staff to the driver of a Cambridge-Bletchley service for the section to Bedford (St John's). A study of the platforms reveals that the Cambridge-bound one is constructed of wood, and the other partially stone flags and the remainder in wood, which would suggest that the passing loop was added at a later date. Lighting is still by oil lamp (1962!). *2587*

Below Blunham, Bedfordshire; Class 108, 10.45 am Cambridge-Oxford, 21 March 1962.

This is a much more substantial station than Willington, although still lit by oil. My first new car – 2 XPA – is visible in the station approach. I am going on to the Mildenhall branch and Newmarket. *2588*

Broom Junction, Warwickshire; Class 100, 1.32 pm Birmingham (New Street)-Evesham, 11 June 1962.
This line formed a loop from the Midland's West of England main line between Ashchurch and Barnt Green, and some freight trains were sent this way. The passenger service was withdrawn between Ashchurch and Evesham in June 1963. By that time it had become just a shuttle, with buses replacing the trains from Redditch in October 1962, because of the condition of the permanent way. Now electric trains connect Lichfield and Birmingham with Redditch. 3053

Left Ynys, Gwynedd; Derby 'Lightweight', 3.40 pm Pwllheli-Llandudno Junction, 22 May 1962.
I discuss this scene in the introductory text. *AL1059*

Below Levisham, North Yorkshire; Class 101, 10.23 am York-Whitby, 1 May 1964. This station was closed between 1965 and 1973 and is now served by the North Yorkshire Moors Railway. At the time of this picture double-track started from here northwards, but otherwise it looks much the same today. *3143*

Bassenthwaite Lake, Cumbria; Derby 'Lightweight', Workington-Keswick, 15 August 1964.
Because of the development of the Cumbrian coast for industry, the A66 needed to be widened from the M6, and on the shore of Bassenthwaite Lake it absorbed the railway, which closed west of Keswick in 1966. 3301

Kilkerran, Strathclyde; Class 120, Stranraer Town-Glasgow (St Enoch), 26 May 1964.
I talk about this view in the introductory text (page 87). 3196

Right Barnard Castle, County Durham; Class 101, 4.34 pm Darlington-Penrith, 3 June 1960.
Barnard Castle was the most significant station between Darlington and Kirkby Stephen, where the tracks divided for Tebay and Penrith, both on the West Coast Main Line, and to this point came branches from Bishop Auckland and Middleton-in-Teesdale. *2049*

Below Alton Heights, Strathclyde; Class 101, Coalburn-Stonehouse ECS, 20 May 1964.
Do observe the nice Caledonian Railway signal box with two 'pulpits' on which the signalman stands to exchange the tokens with the driver for the single lines. *3174*

INDEX